Douglas Duncan

Douglas Duncan

A MEMORIAL PORTRAIT

EDITED BY

ALAN JARVIS

UNIVERSITY OF TORONTO PRESS

© University of Toronto Press 1974

Toronto and Buffalo

Printed in Canada

ISBN 0-8020-1977-3

LC 72-97526

Contents

List of Illustrations

Foreword

To become a legend in one's own lifetime must be a slightly exasperating experience; Douglas Duncan regarded the whole business as jocose. If he were to know that a book was being written about him his reaction would be of gently cynical amusement: the one creature he would never take seriously was himself.

Nevertheless, a book has been written, and a few of the many people whose lives he affected have contributed to it. I have no doubt that more will be written about Douglas, especially his relation with David Milne but, meanwhile, this book – a memorial, not a definitive biography – must suffice, and I wish to give wholehearted thanks to those people who have contributed papers and to those many others who do not appear in print but whose unsparing help and advice has been invaluable.

Special tribute must be paid to Mrs J.P. Barwick, Douglas' sister, who coped admirably with the immensely difficult job not only of sorting out Douglas' estate but of arranging so thoughtfully and sensitively the dispersal of the collection of works of art, books, binding tools, etc, throughout Canada: truly a service to the nation. I know she would wish me to acknowledge the great help she received from Mr Cecil Troy, for some years assistant to Douglas at the Picture Loan Society.

One very important aspect of Douglas' work may not appear with sufficient clarity in these pages: his unsparing giving of his time and (not always robust) energy to the encouragement of other collectors. The most notable, of course, was the late J.S. Maclean; there are many other people collecting, on a lesser scale but with an equal passion, whom Douglas helped. Many Canadian art galleries sought – and always received – his advice. Most notable among these is the Art Gallery of Ontario and Mrs Peggy Lownsborough of the Women's Committee who has told me of how Douglas would resolutely remain silent when he felt that his opinion was not relevant. Max Merkur has told me of Douglas lining up four or five Milne paintings against the Picture Loan walls and asking him to rank them in order of quality and importance. Merkur maintains that Douglas even submitted David Milne jr to the same treatment! *Si non e vero e ben trovato.*

The essay on pages 7 to 13 was written for the catalogue of the Duncan exhibition. It is reprinted here, with some alterations, by kind permission of the Chairman and Trustees of the Gallery and of the Director, Dr Jean Boggs.

Publication of the book has been made possible by the assistance of a grant from the Canada Council.

DOUGLAS DUNCAN

The Right Honourable
Lester B. Pearson

Remarks delivered at the opening of the Douglas Duncan exhibition
at the National Gallery of Canada, Ottawa, 4 March 1971

There are many here with a much greater claim than I have to speak on such an occasion: because of their closer association with Douglas Duncan, whom we honour tonight; their greater knowledge of his life and work; or because of their own contribution to the arts for which Douglas Duncan did so much himself. Not the least of his contribution is this magnificent gift of pictures from the Duncan Estate to the National Gallery; a gift which has also been made possible by the generosity, the interest, and untiring work of his sister, Mrs Jack Barwick.

I have always admired and appreciated the unique qualities and the creative work of Douglas Duncan. I had the privilege of meeting him during those days, so long ago, when, as a student at Victoria College, he was a member of a small coterie of stimulating and intelligent undergraduates, interested in college activities that went beyond football and proms (a group that included one dark-haired and singularly attractive co-ed whom at the time I was trying to persuade to join the faculty wives). Indeed, she should be speaking instead of me, as one who has always valued so greatly her friendship with Douglas begun in those years.

Douglas Duncan was a rare person. He gave meaning to those shop-worn words 'unique' and 'distinction.' It is a depressing reflection on our times and on today's *mores* that his constructive work and his dedicated service to the cultural, the non-material, development of our nation's life is so much less known, or less generally appreciated, than that of many lesser persons doing smaller things which were more newsworthy because they were spectacular or controversial. But, as so often happens, the importance of his life, and his service to the arts to which he dedicated that life, is being more widely recognized now that he has gone.

His life span covered the unlikely combination of Kalamazoo, Cornwall, Paris, and, of course, Toronto, which became the centre of his interests and activities, and where he is best known.

Bookbinding – with work of beauty and style – was his first artistic love and expression. It led naturally to the collection of rare and good books from which more than one library – but especially that at the University of Toronto – has benefited.

He will, however, be remembered best for his Picture Loan Society – so unique a concept and so uniquely his own, and through which he did so much to spread the gospel of appreciation of Canadian painting, and encourage and help those who painted. No young artist who ever approached him was ignored or rejected. The operation and the influence of the Society was – as Alan Jarvis has written – 'Douglas Duncan's "intangible legacy," ' while his collection of paintings, now so widely distributed, was its tangible expression. All Canadians who love painting are his debtors – and especially those who themselves were enabled and encouraged by him to paint and persevere.

The way the Society carried on, how as well as what it operated, reflects well the kind of person Douglas Duncan was: this tall rumpled, unconventional, and to many, I suppose, disconcerting man. In a time of bowing down to corporate and organizational efficiency, which can be so depressing in many ways, he was supremely and wonderfully unorganized and unorthodox. His business 'methods,' which are now becoming a Canadian legend, rejected C O D for P Y R – Payment by *your* Request. However, if you pressed too hard for a bill, you were in danger of being cut off the list of clients. Even today there must be hundreds of people wondering how much they owe Douglas Duncan – and I am reducing the debt now simply to money. In this frightening age of computers and psychiatric couches, one can gain comfort and hope from Douglas Duncan's insistence: 'Thank God, I have no system!' 'What this country needs – I believe Douglas Duncan would agree with me – is 'more unopened letters and uncashed cheques'; more 'third floor backs on 3 Charles Street West' even if it means fewer skyscrapers for super-banks.

He was modest and unassuming in everything he did – to the point of self-effacement. His satisfaction came from what he could do for art and artists, not what he could do for himself, by collecting paintings – or anything else. It is not always so, even in the cultural world.

Norman Endicott, in writing of Douglas Duncan, once said, 'The way you hear about "the Mellon Collection" you'd think Mr Mellon himself had painted it. There's none of that nonsense about the "Duncan Collection."' Douglas once said that he merely considered himself 'a casual collector.' Indeed he seemed to regard with suspicion any formal concept of 'collection' and 'collector.' Alan Jarvis quotes him as saying 'A collector is the sort of person who owns works by six members of the Group of Seven and lives in torment until he can fill the gap with a purchase of the seventh.' That kind of collector,

today, would not free himself from torment even after achieving his seventh; what will a white paper on taxation eventually do to any of his pictures? Lorenzo the Magnificent would not find it too easy to be a public benefactor and a blessed patron of the arts in the federal state of Canada in the last half of the twentieth century.

Douglas Duncan's 'casual' collection of paintings – including those by which the National Gallery will now so greatly benefit – as practically every gallery in the country has benefited – is a roll call of Canadian artistic talent.

The paintings of Milne are, of course, a major part of the collection, but they are only a part. Douglas was as catholic, if discriminating, in his appreciation of art as he was generous in his encouragement and assistance of artists. Yet for Milne he had a special attachment. I share his feeling for the work of this strange but authentic genius who put beauty above all material things.

The man who has so greatly enriched our artistic life by his perception and his generosity has thereby enriched our whole national life. In doing so, he has, I hope, helped us to realize that there is far more to national development than a seven per cent annual

5   Lester B. Pearson

increase in G N P; and far more to personal development than reaching the highest income tax bracket or the lowest golf score.

I am very privileged tonight to pay this humble tribute to a quiet, unselfish Canadian who 'wrought better than he knew.'

Alan Jarvis

On the occasion of the opening of an exhibition, at the Willistead Gallery in Windsor in October 1967, of a selection of works which he owned, Douglas Duncan, to the astonishment of a good many people, walked to the lectern and spoke on his own behalf. The astonishment arose because Duncan had always been self-effacing to the point of invisibility and had cocooned himself in a *persona* of shyness which had become legendary.

Slowly surveying this handsomely presented exhibition, Douglas announced, 'This is not a collection ... it is an accretion.' As always he was using language with precision and he spoke quietly and calmly but with authority. His noun was perfectly accurate. He was not a collector as the word is normally understood. He never beat about the bushes and hedgerows seeking bargains or finds. Instead he hived up at 3 Charles Street West, Toronto, and the artists (and collectors of the conventional mould) came to him, trudging the three flights of stairs with their portfolios or canvases under their arms.

They were greeted by a quietly affable man who, more often than not, squatted on his hunkers – a position he found comfortable and which allowed his visitors to see over his head to the important things, the pictures – with a cigarette poised between elegant, attenuated fingers. They were greeted by a dispassionate D M D. (I shall use this trigram henceforth because it was the way he liked to sign his sporadic letters or dedicate the countless books he felt the young needed for their edification and which he distributed like a one-man Gideon society.) If or when they presented their work his judgment would be direct, considered, and frank – sometimes even brutal – but almost always of impeccable taste. I use the word almost because I was privileged to share with him the choosing of works to be included in the Willistead show, and from time to time, after long contemplation, we agreed that certain works did not merit hanging alongside the obviously first rate. On a few occasions – usually out of sheer kindliness – D M D had adopted young artists of promise, promise which they never fulfilled. Without either recrimination or regret, their work was shifted to the 'study collection.'

Although outwardly cool and calm, D M D entertained what Bertrand Russell once defined as the most important thing in life – intense personal relationships. No one who was fortunate enough to come close to Douglas would deny that the phrase applied perfectly to him. Perhaps his greatest gift to mankind and to Canadian art was his intense empathy.

As with all civilized people he did not suffer fools gladly but he did so patiently and, of course, graciously. Nevertheless he was sometimes provoked to what one of his favourite writers, Max Beerbohm, called the silent curl of the nostril accompanied by a sharply barbed riposte.

This present exhibition is visible proof of his dedication to the proposition that art must be shared, especially Canadian art by the whole of the Canadian people. At the back of his multi-faceted mind there stood the concept that works in his possession should ultimately become public property. They now have.

The myth that D M D was the indulged scion of a wealthy family is quite false. He lived modestly, sometimes austerely, and his lack of interest in clothes and food became part of the Duncan legend in the public mind. I travelled seven thousand miles with him through France, Bavaria, and northern Italy during the summer of 1938 and, to the best of my recollection, he lived entirely on *chocolat liégeois*.

D M D never wanted either wealth or any indulgences for himself, yet his generosity to others was astonishing. I once saw him slip a Craven A box across

David Milne, Douglas Duncan, and Alan Jarvis
'Three poor pictures with their respective artists; all six out of focus. DBM, DMD and AJ at the entrance to Pretty Channel, Six-Mile Lake, Sept. 2, 1936.'

a restaurant table to a young Canadian artist: the packet contained ten one-hundred-dollar bills. I have, however, seen him say to another young artist he felt was being importunate, 'This has got to stop!' The words were spoken graciously, but very firmly. Duncan was kindliness personified but he was never foolish.

Beneath his outward austerity there lay a deeply rooted, deliciously subtle sense of humour. (I am happy to possess initialled copies of his favourite writers: Samuel Butler, Max Beerbohm, Aldous Huxley, John Collier.) A splendid example that comes to mind out of a virtual sea of recollections of D M D is his first encounter with David Milne. We had gone together to the first Mellors-Laing exhibition in 1934 and we had both been captivated by the paintings. Milne, too, had become something of a legendary figure in the minds of the tiny number of people who at that period had heard of him. He was said to be a recluse who was hiding himself away on the shores of a remote Muskoka lake in order, it was quite falsely put about, to keep free of all influence. (Milne demolished this nonsense when later he remarked to me, 'Why, you could see a painting through the crack of a door … and be influenced for

The Maple Blooms on Hiram's Farm
DAVID MILNE
oil on canvas, 1933
actual size 20″ by 28″
reproduced by permission of the
London Public Library and Art Museum

life.') We were sufficiently captivated by the Milne painting that we resolved to see the mythical character in the flesh, and so we made our way, by car and canoe, to Six-Mile Lake in the summer of 1935. When we had hauled the canoe ashore on a bare point of rock on which stood a small tar-paper shack, Milne emerged and walked shyly down toward us. With mock solemnity and a courtly bow, D M D said: 'We have just come to burn a little incense.' That was the beginning of a relationship which was to become the most remarkable in the history of Canadian art. However, that story can only be told in proper detail elsewhere. It must suffice, in the present context, to make two brief quotations from the correspondence between D M D and H.O. McCurry and Kathleen Fenwick that is preserved in the National Gallery archives. The first is a letter from Harry McCurry to D M D: '… I do not think you need feel too squeamish about bringing any first rate Milne to our attention. True, we cannot overload ourselves with him but, looking to the future, we are anxious to build up the best representation of his work that we can and I feel if you know this and will continue to help us, we shall be doing just that …' (20 January 1948). I quote the second excerpt to illustrate the

felicitous rapport that existed between D M D and the National Gallery. It is from a letter to McCurry from Douglas: '… Milne and I started to weed out the pictures. We burned forty of the dingiest of 1909-11, and then gave up; deciding that since the residue was to be offered to the National Gallery, that institution might as well take on the intimidating responsibility of selection. The few pictures of 1917 and later are mostly dregs – anything of value having been retained with, I hope, impeccable taste … However there are many passable things – and extremely curious in their violence – among the pictures of 1912-16. But they are very different from the work of 1917 on and mostly inferior to it: so we felt they should be, so to speak, sterilized, and stored somewhere only for reference and curiosity.' (22 April 1939)

It would be a great mistake to allow D M D to be associated solely with Milne. However much this great painter preoccupied him and absorbed a great proportion of his time – by dint of working long hours, frequently excessively long, to the detriment of his never robust health – Douglas managed to aid and promote an extraordinarily large number of artists. These were mostly young Canadians such as Harold Town and Robert Hedrick, but his interest and sponsorship was extended also to established artists such as Will Ogilvie and Paraskeva Clark. It is worth noting that the first exhibition held at the Picture Loan Society showed the work of Carl Schaefer.

At its inception the Picture Loan was a society – based on the British Picture Hire organization which H.G. Kettle had seen and studied in London. Together with Norah McCullough and D M D, Kettle helped found the Society in 1936, with premises at 3 Charles Street West on the third floor over a dancing school and an accordion school, both of which provided an incongruous background for the galleries D M D organized. He had in the same suite his own elegantly untidy bed-sitter and bookbinding place and, a little later on, a darkroom in a dank closet. Others (Harold Stacey and myself, initially) occupied space until the slow accretion of works of art inexorably drove us out. It was not very long after its formation that the Society between D M D and vice versa, if only because he alone had the time and the resources to maintain it, and in addition he had the obsessive love of his cause to spur him to endless hours of sheer donkey work: framing, cutting mats, packing

and unpacking crates, making up advertisements and so on.

In 1939, D M D made the last of his hitherto annual summer-long trips to his tiny but efficient *pied-à-terre* in Paris. After that date his life was divided in varying proportions between the Picture Loan, Milne, his Muskoka cabin, and a modest amount of travel to other galleries in Canada and the United States. I have never been able to understand how he resisted the pull of Paris and Europe. When he was asked, the reply was silence and a rather glazed stare over one's left shoulder at some remote horizon.

The Picture Loan was, naturally, in its early years a reflection of the Canadian Group of Painters. In previous years D M D had shown great interest in the Group of Seven, especially LeMoine FitzGerald, and the non-member, Emily Carr. As time went on, the D M D / P L S showed an increasing interest in the younger up-coming artists and in some of the mature but rather obscure painters such as Borduas.

It must not be thought that D M D cared solely for a domestic product. Far from it. He wandered afield from time to time with, for example, 'Scottie Wilson and the unique British genius, Wyndham Lewis. The latter rewarded D M D for his help, while he, Lewis, was something of a displaced person, with a vicious caricature of an aesthete-benefactor.

D M D's wholly personal collection reflected his great catholicity. It ranged from a Spanish Romanesque Madonna and Child in polychromed wood to a heroic Bourdelle bronze, from a Picasso lithograph to a Käthe Kollwitz drawing.

Although he could well be described as an eccentric, and infuriatingly wayward in a good many of his daily doings, especially in his neglect of such boring matters as keeping accounts and depositing cheques, his life was a full and rich one and, of course, eminently civilized. He was deeply interested in music, theatre, and films, and allocated a fair, sometimes indulgent, amount of time to these interests. He was a passionate collector of wild flowers and a naturist in the classical sense of the word, peeling off all his clothes at the first peep of sunshine.

I lived abroad for some fourteen years but very fortunately I was able to return to Canada at least once a year, sometimes much more frequently. Always my first call was on D M D. Over the years it was fascinating, amusing, and not a little dismaying to watch 3 Charles Street West become increasingly cluttered, dusty, and – we must face it – chaotic. There were many times when D M D himself could not find where he had put some work, others when, with a sort of built-in radar, he would unearth the work in question from the stacks of paintings, drawings, mats, and packing crates. If one expressed surprise at these performances, D M D would smile gently and mutter, 'You know there is a law of physics that explains all that.'

There is no law of physics, or indeed of psychology, that can adequately explain D M D. But, if you seek his monument, look about you – not just at the 'Duncan Accretion' but at the endless manifestations of his influence on the art scene in Canada. Above all, talk to the people who knew him. Statistically, he probably infuriated as often as he captivated but there are few Canadians who did not revere him and a great many who grew to love him. I suppose there is a law of something that explains that.

Northrop Frye

The opening page of Evelyn Waugh's *The Loved One* introduces an Englishman, exiled in California, who is trying to make sense of an article in *Horizon* on Scottie Wilson. Scottie Wilson was, of course, one of that very large group of painters whose careers owed much of their success to a friendly push from Douglas Duncan at a crucial stage. The *Horizon* article speaks of Douglas as 'a refined and charming man.' The author of the article obviously did not know him, and the phrase is oddly out of keeping with the general tone of the article. It looks as though the phrase had been supplied by Scottie Wilson himself, or perhaps that he had insisted on some such phrase being inserted.

If this is true, as it may well not be, it would be a good example of the way in which those who were fond of or grateful to Douglas might struggle for phrases to describe him, only to have the right one elude them. Of course he was a refined and charming man, but so have a lot of other people been who never got anywhere near being Douglas Duncan. The phrase suggests something of a dilettante, which he was far from being. My own association with him professionally was through Victoria College, where my wife was for years chairman of the Art

Committee. The year's activity usually began by getting hold of Douglas. When suggestions for exhibitions did not come from him, they almost always referred to painters he knew about and had done something to help. Whenever he spoke, his encyclopaedic knowledge came out in a context of complete simplicity and candour. He seemed to be a still centre in the swirling egotisms and aggressions and intrigues which characterize the art world in all cities, and his critical judgments had the kind of impartiality that only a genuine sympathy can produce.

We all tend to like what is like ourselves: if we try to be objective, we may eventually come to like what is like our best self. Canadian history and politics have always been polarized between two tendencies: one aggressive, exploratory, and romantic; the other reflective, observant, and pastoral. The same polarization occurs in Canadian literature and painting. In painting the aggressive and romantic tendency is represented by Thomson, the Group of Seven, and Emily Carr; in the second group I think particularly of David Milne and LeMoine Fitzgerald. Tolerant and catholic as Douglas' tastes were, he had a strong temperamental affinity with the second

group, and he had an extraordinary genius for discovering painters of crisp, delicate, and precise drawing and colouring, whose work was close to a kind of pictorial calligraphy.

I never go into Alumni Hall in Victoria College, where he had arranged so many exhibitions, without thinking of him, in the centre of a great mass of paintings, with his little piece of green felt for twisting the screws, hanging the pictures, arranging them, disregarding the very considerable pain that his disc trouble often gave him. It is a picture of extraordinary selflessness: hard, conscientious, and almost anonymous work done so that the artist would have another exhibition to chalk up on his record and Victoria students would have pictures to look at. Paradoxically, the memory of him is far more vivid than the memory of even the finest of the pictures.

Norman Endicott

For the last thirty years of his life Douglas was thought of by most of those who knew him publicly – painters and people interested in the arts – as a collector of Canadian paintings whose principal occupation was the Picture Loan Society. But I think one can safely say that, almost up to the founding of that Society in 1936, Douglas' strongest interests were literature, some biographical aspects of history as revealed in literature, and music, to which he listened with critical absorption. And it was of course as a fine bookbinder that he set up a small studio in Toronto in 1928.

In his school years extremely shy and self-conscious, and not given to games (partly as the result of a dubious constitution, early uncertain health, and illness), he read a great deal, but mostly in his own chosen areas; by the time he was sixteen his interests were already definitely directed toward France. Reading Dumas, at the age of eleven in a corner behind the sofa, and later other books, including some French memoirs (mostly in translation) led to a lively historical, and then architectural, interest in Blois, or Chambord, or Chenonceaux, years before he could visit the places themselves. Perhaps it was early reading of Scott, not Dumas, that led him to visit and indeed revisit the romantic ruins of Chateau-Gaillard, the castle of Richard Côeur-de-Lion, not far from Rouen.

His career at the University of Toronto, after a first unsuccessful year in commerce and finance (a preposterous choice for one of his tastes, temperament, and abilities) was academically lazy, and very undistinguished. His own ironical tentative description for *Torontonensis* ran: 'After an impeccable career at U T S [University of Toronto Schools] he glided softly through his college years, knowing at the end of the fourth year several persons of each sex. Is absorbed chiefly in books and music.' Already his comments and his letters, the latter always more formulated and telling than his conversation, showed an ambivalent combination of extreme romanticism and dry and ironic observation, or amusement, appreciated by, and largely kept for, his more intimate friends. At Bigwin Inn, with his family, he escaped from sports, or the boredom of non-conversation, in a canoe with a book, and named an island L'Isle Joyeuse in tribute to Debussy. But he could also write for the possible loan of a pair of white flannels in considerably stylized phrases suggesting to the recipient what was thought at home about his own introspectiveness: 'to my surprise and faint irritation I found that the pair I had brought with me ... can now no more be useful save as a source of wistful reflections. They were old and were originally narrow, no doubt, but with the years they have drawn more and more into themselves, so that now, even by endangering modesty and – more important – impairing the elegance of my waistline, I am unable to make them approach, even remotely, the ground.'

The liking for the ridiculous situation and absurd image, and for the ironic – reflected in his enjoyment of the writings and *Notebooks* of Samuel Butler – was part of Douglas' temperament all his life, and became more apparent as the romantic side paled. In his earlier years the romantic was more obvious, and included not only a strong interest in the Middle Ages and the Renaissance, but also in Pre-Raphaelitism and the literature and art of the eighteen nineties – not excluding Beardsley, hardly in the ordinary sense romantic. But the affectionate satire of Max Beerbohm's *Rossetti and his Circle* (not long published) was very congenial, and obviously in the nineteen twenties (to say nothing of in Victoria College) it would have needed a preternaturally pure and belated aesthete to take Pre-Raphaelitism, or Wilde, or *Axël*, or even Pater with entire solemnity. Of Max Beerbohm himself, however (or rather of early Max Beerbohm) Douglas could write: 'I like Max very much in spite of his atmosphere of extreme clever insincerity. I feel amused, not repelled, when he says "That was indeed a fine piece of prose – but don't let it distract you from my theme etc." ' Looking at a proof of the then customary graduation photograph, phrases from Pater's famous or notorious description of La Gioconda came easily to his mind. He could hardly hope that his face showed very explicitly 'strange thoughts and fantastic reveries and exquisite passions,' but he noted that, because he had been up too often and too late, 'the eyelids are a little weary,' and added that a good photographer, unlike Leonardo, could probably do something about such a blemish.

Graduation somehow achieved, he was faced with not knowing what he wanted to do, coupled with an extreme unwillingness to accept the prospect of 'working his way up to the top' in the business of his father (S.F. Duncan of Provincial Paper). Also, a number of his friends were going, or had gone, to Europe for study, and he himself had had an exciting taste of Europe in 1922, on a visit with his family.

(Though he was a Protestant this had included kissing the Pope's ring, an occasion which brought out a characteristic comment. The stone, he wrote back, was a beautiful colour, but exasperatingly he had had to move on 'before he could get a really good look at it.') The prospect seemed gloomy. For five or six months he demonstrated, with some strain, that he could be a conscientious young business man, and tried to consider other prospects 'only at the most frigid distance.' Then, to his great surprise, parental support came for a year in France. And so 'I leave a week from Monday for Paris ... Of course I've wanted to for – oh – always.' His parents (rather innocently indeed!) 'didn't want him to study too assiduously,' and so he planned to enjoy living in France; seeing cathedrals and chateaux and villages in the country, people and museums (and Paris) in Paris, and finding out about France and French culture in a Sorbonne course for strangers, if this course was not 'too appallingly superficial' – which it was after a few weeks.

Paris itself was not, though it was a little exhausting: 'I have in these hundred days walked many hundred miles ... I live largely on porridge and apple sauce and choux de Bruxelles and petit pois and corn bread, with occasional incursions into the animal kingdom, more for variety than pleasure.' Not hard up, but with a very modest amount to live on, and so eager an interest in concerts and opera and trips to Chartres or Rouen that only daily frugalities allowed him to enjoy what he really most wanted, he could write (with some intentional flamboyance): 'Last Monday evening at the Opéra was the first time I'd worn my tuxedo since I left the Mauretania. And that was only because I asked Miss Douglas to go to the revival of Gluck's *Alceste* and got seats where "tenue de soirée est de riguer." and [even] there in the midst of bedizened dowager duchesses so decayed but flaming with rouge and diamonds, the seats are only $1.50 plus tips and programmes.'

From the first, living in France naturally extended and deepened Douglas' feelings for and knowledge of mediaeval and Renaissance art and architecture. But music and literature were still primary. Music meant many concerts and also the buying of a great many gramophone records. Literature meant at first buying just books, then buying first editions and finely printed books, and then beginning to concentrate on more complete collections of certain favourite authors. The presence in Douglas' library,

after his death, of a copy of *Robinson Crusoe* presented to him by his mother on his eighth birthday and in very fine physical shape (though to my knowledge much read) suggests that, while a bibliographer can be made, a bibliophile is usually born. At all events, when Douglas returned from France he brought back with him quite a few cases of books, and from that year (1928) until 1934 or 1935 bought a great many more. In the latter year he made a classified list of his purchases in the previous eight or nine years. Like his later collection of paintings and drawings, the list is very impressive for someone with so modest an income. 'Art,' 'Architecture and Travel,' 'Modern Design,' 'Bookbinding and Bibliography,' take quite a few pages, and a large number of substantial and authoritative books are listed – the library, if not of a scholar, of a very knowledgeable and serious amateur, in the original good sense of the word. There are books on Romanesque sculpture and architecture and iconography; books on Chartres, Rouen, Amiens, Lyon, and other cathedrals and churches; books on stained glass, wrought iron, mediaeval ivories, borough and monastic seals, Florentine wall frescoes; books on modern design and architecture; Gordon Craig's and other handsome books on the theatre, etc, etc. There are quite a number of beautiful or interesting illustrated books, among them Beardsley's *Morte D'Arthure*, A Virgil of 1529 with woodcuts, the Cranach Press edition of Virgil's *Ecologues* with illustrations by Maillol, two or three Kelmscott Press books and quite a few from the Nonesuch Press, the Golden Cockerel Press *Four Gospels* illustrated by Eric Gill, many books on, and reproductions of, Blake. Books on bookbindings are naturally much in evidence; one of the handsomest, M.J. Husung's *Bucheinbände aus der Preussischen Staatsbibliothek zu Berlin*, too expensive for his own purse at that time, was characteristically chosen as a Christmas present from his father.

Modern English and French literature runs to hundreds of titles. Buying first editions had really begun in 1927. By the end of 1931 Douglas noted that, counting the much-corrected typescript of D.H. Lawrence's *Women in Love*, for which he paid what was for him the totally unusual and reckless sum of £300 (I remember an evening's discussion as to whether this was madness), his collection of Proust, Lawrence, Beerbohm, Norman Douglas, and De la Mare (this an exception to his usual interests) had cost him over $3000. From then until 1935 or 1936 (after which time buying pictures took over) he extended his collections both of these writers and of others who (except for André Gide and Samuel Butler) did not hold quite so special a place in his reading: Richard Aldington, Aldous Huxley, Richard Hughes, John Collier (an undervalued wit and writer of whom Douglas had some mss as well as books), Lacretelle, Wilde, Virginia Woolf, Faulkner. The Beerbohm collection contained corrected typescript and manuscript material; some of the Butler items are very interesting. Two of these, Butler's own copies of his translation of the *Iliad*, and of *Erewhon Revisited*, with lists of those to whom he wanted copies sent, have gone, at Douglas' wish, to the Butler collection in St John's College, Cambridge. Other special items are now in the University of Toronto library, to which most of the literary collection, and much else, including many art books, books on bookbinding, etc, have also been given. The collections of Lawrence, Proust, and Beerbohm are no doubt the most important; but the total of books, pamphlets, and periodicals is also substantial.

Of course he also, as he wrote, 'looked at pictures indefatigably' in Paris. One experience of 1926 was described in an exceptionally enthusiastic style. He was on a brief visit to the Louvre when, 'after having seemed for half an hour unable to escape from primitive anatomy … I happened to discover a staircase. There was a guardian dreamily surveying me from a chair, but I started up the steps, furtively watching him out of the corner of my eye. Oddly enough he seemed officially indifferent to my explorations, and finally I discovered the Camondo Collection. Is that what you saw a year ago? … All the rest of the day I was "excited inside" about the Monets there. I vaguely remember a lot of Degas and Manet and Sisley, but in the few minutes I was there it was certain of the Monets that made such an impression. I am curious to see whether I now like whatever there may be in Luxembourg – whether, in other words, it was a case of the Grace of God – you know, like "getting religion." ' *Buying* French paintings. impressionist or later, was of course out of the question; the first significant contemporary print Douglas bought, in 1929, was a Picasso lithograph. But no doubt the conflict between bibliophile and picture collector was already incipient. On one occasion he knew that a book he much wanted was coming up for auction at the Salle Drouot. Hesitatingly he drew out as much as he could from a

then not very flush bank account, in order to bid. The book went for much more. On the way home he thought of a Paul Klee drawing he had several times looked at admiringly in the window of a small gallery near his apartment. Why not? But he had not pounced in time; it too was gone.

By the end of his first year in Paris, Douglas had decided on fine bookbinding as his chosen profession. 'I should so love to be able to *make* something,' he wrote to his father. 'To work with one's head *and* one's hands seems ideal … there would be such satisfaction in feeling that I had, out of some printed leaves, cardboard, leather and gold leaf, made something attractive, and made it with my own hands, not indirectly, as part of a company.' So for two more years he remained in Paris to learn his craft, returning in subsequent summers for further lessons. His teachers were recognized masters; Monsieur Noulhac for the practical work of cutting, sewing, glueing, pasting, paring, and covering, and Monsieur Domont for tooling, gilding, and other decorative techniques. The latter, eighty and still very active, with black fez and 'whiskers like the knight in *The Looking Glass*,' 'was a fiend at detecting a curve in the end of a straight line,' and would keep him repeating lozenge designs on a curved back for hours or for days 'because it is good practice.'

In the fall of 1928 he returned to Toronto, not without some reluctance, to set up as a bookbinder. 'I shall hate to leave [Paris],' he wrote, 'for I would rather live here than anywhere else. And hope to, some day. Or at least I should like to reverse the method of Miss Lahey, the incomparable binder of the Morgan Library, who spends the summer months working in Paris. I should like to go back to Canada for June, July, August, September, and perhaps October.' About bookbinding as an adequate source of income he had no delusions. 'At first,' he wrote, 'and for some time I imagine, my binding will only keep me in chocolate peppermints. Dividends etc provides me with a fairly certain background – $2300 about.' Since he not only looked like an intellectual or artist but was often somewhat rumpled in appearance, it was not surprising that the local grocer from whom he bought one or two eggs at a time (to use the whites in gilding), took a while to realize that his customer was not an artist down to his last penny.

Toronto was not a good place in which to practise fine binding, and some of his commissions were a little painfully ironic to one who associated fine binding with fine printing and literary quality. ('Will you please bind a book for my coffee table' one young woman asked. 'What book?' 'Oh, I don't care.' She was steered elsewhere.) But his bindings continued to be meticulous in workmanship and elegant in style, the decorative motifs sometimes traditional, sometimes derived from experiments, or from stone friezes and medallions, or wrought-iron grilles which he had photographed in Europe. The end papers, too, English, French, and American, are strikingly varied, and sometimes brilliant. Moreover his frustrations must have been in part compensated for by the invitations he received to exhibit his work both at home and abroad, as for instance in Paris in 1937 at the Exposition internationale – a just recognition of books that are beautiful as well as professional in craftsmanship. After his death Douglas' binding tools – some impossible to match in quality today – were presented to the University of Toronto Press, where they are used for special bindings.

In 1936 the Picture Loan Society was founded, with Douglas at first one of a committee and then, after a while, solely responsible. This soon redirected practically all special book buying into picture buying, and gradually his own profession was put aside for the time-consuming activities of a gallery and exhibitions. He bound no books after 1944. His own aims as a collector were expressed in a brief statement, based on an interview, in *Canadian Art*, May-June 1961. One sentence runs: 'I have no mission ... I have merely assembled a large collection of oils, water colours, drawings, and prints that I have liked and that I continue to enjoy ...' Save for a few pictures sold, without profit, to the National Gallery and the Art Gallery of Ontario, I think he never resold pictures he had himself bought, so that, as his collection grew, so did the storage problems. Until his father's death he had lived in the large family home, where, as the family and its activities dwindled, he had taken over more and more rooms (the billiard room being especially useful). When the house was sold in 1964, he moved into two adjoining apartments, but soon overflowed into a third, all three naturally equipped with hardly necessary kitchens, save that one could be used as a dark room for photography. He made an attempt to house the framed pictures neatly in racks, the unframed ones on shelves or in wooden boxes. He intended to buy more bookcases for his books. But at the time of his death two of the apartments still presented an engulfing scene of shelves, stacks, trunks, boxes, and cartons – primarily of books, pictures, and gramophone records, but also of correspondence, old programmes, Christmas cards going back to childhood, and various objects accumulated over a long time.

For many years, in all weathers and in at least three of the four seasons, Douglas spent quite a few weekends, and in the summer longer periods when he could, in Muskoka. There were also expeditions to the handsomer shores of Georgian Bay. With the pride of an amateur, he took a full and competent share in building his own cabin, carefully planned, and even painted a gallery gray inside. But as usual making no distinction between himself and others as victims of procrastination, the pipes to bring water to his sink were still not connected twenty years later, despite the necessity of carrying pails of water after more than once suffering from a slipped disc. Unlike four-fifths of today's 'cottagers,' who, when not convivial, spend their time making a noise and stink in high-powered motor boats, Douglas had only a canoe, and was an indefatigable rambler and looker.

Not in any scientific sense a naturalist, he was nevertheless very observant and knowledgeable about wild flowers and ferns – some of which he brought back to chosen locations in his own woods – and in his searches for these he came to know the maple and beech valleys, and the cedar swamps of at least a few miles of Muskoka in topographical detail, as well as with a most accurate eye for every effect of shape and texture, especially, perhaps, the more delicate: lichen on old logs, maidenhair spleenwort in a crevice of rock, the shades of colour in a hillside of hepaticas in early spring. The photographs he made of veined rocks and whaleback islets in Georgian Bay, stumps and roots in the water in Algonquin Park, patterns of lines and shadows in winter woods, or, at close range, of his colony of large round-leaved orchids in full but delicate bloom, are very good by any standards. Naturally David Milne's feeling, for the same effects and landscape was a link between them, but Douglas also liked Milne's comments on his *Hepaticas*: 'Do you like flowers? So do I. But I never paint them. I didn't see the hepaticas. I saw, instead, an arrangement of the lines, spaces, hues, values, and relations that I habitually use. That is, I saw one of my own pictures.' Unlike the Group of Seven, Milne did not reach for epic rhythms or alien harshness and grandeur, but painted like an intimate and old inhabitant of the scene, and this, without making any invidious comparisons, appealed, I think, to Douglas. But Milne also painted from whatever might be in front of him, from paper bags as willingly as from hepaticas, and Douglas did not buy pictures for their sentimental associations.

After an exhausting afternoon expedition in the hot and often mosquitoed woods or swamps looking for orchids, and a late supper with us, his neighbours and fellow ramblers, Douglas would make his way by flashlight through the woods to his own cabin and stretch out his six-foot-three to listen to some records – from Monteverdi's *Orfeo* to Strauss, Stravinsky, or Prokofieff, or (old favourites) Debussy's songs or his string quartet. One summer he read the interminable Goncourt *Journal* (in the nine-volume presentation copy he had bought in Paris many years before!) until he got 'housemaid's elbow,' as he said, from lying propped up so many late hours. And, at the same time as he enjoyed this remote literary gossip, he also shared the ironical attitude toward the *Journal* felt by the narrator in Proust's *Le Temps retrouvé*. An odd scene this, for Muskoka, Ontario, Canada.

Snow covered swamp, photograph by DMD

Most of what I have been recalling is in some way
related to Douglas as a collector and bibliophile. A
collector with admirable taste and judgment, an
ardent bibliophile, may be a bore, or a man of little
personal feeling or attractiveness of character. Those
who knew Douglas did not think of him first as the
owner of pictures or books or other objects. His best
books are now available in public libraries, his pictures a part of galleries across Canada. Douglas'
friends remember the imaginative thoughtfulness of
his actions, his generosity and invariable awareness
of people as individuals, the sense of humour and the
sense of the absurd which made him good company
as well as a good friend.

Robert Finch

Douglas Duncan arrived in Paris on 9 November 1925. He was twenty-three. He first occupied a room in the Hôtel Jeanne d'Arc, rue Vaneau, where I was already staying. It was a coldish winter but by December we were lucky enough to find, across the way at No 86, a heated apartment. Its flamboyant striped wallpaper, crimson carpeting, and heavy brass bedsteads, then widely prevalent in France, we looked on as an amusing kind of Maupassant setting. In return for a small monthly supplement, we enjoyed the services of Emil, the *garçon d'étage*, who came in to do the cleaning and wash the dishes. On the other hand, if we invited a single guest, the dearth of cutlery proved embarrassing. We introduced nothing new into the apartment except two indispensable pieces of furniture: Douglas, a gramophone, I, a grand piano. In due course we learned of distinguished neighbours. Nadia Boulanger and André Gide had homes in the same street, Matisse lived not far away, and it was only a few blocks from our house to the university. The situation had something slightly symbolic about it, since music, literature, and art were always in the air even when our *chauffage central* was not.

It was like Douglas to obtain at once a large-scale map of the city, which he hung on the wall of his room and unfailingly consulted before setting out on daily excursions, in the process of which, as he himself often stated, he walked literally hundreds of miles. He soon knew where to find every place of interest, especially historic monuments, art galleries, auditoriums, and book-shops; what is more, despite the directional peculiarities of Paris streets, he was able to go anywhere by the most expeditious route. I have known few others, Parisians or not, so thoroughly acquainted with the lay-out of each *arrondissement*.

Like myself, Douglas registered for post-graduate work at the université de Paris but this institution proved as little sympathetic to him as had the University of Toronto. His intention, after following certain preliminary courses, was to have undertaken a 'big subject ... the composition of the government, and the French financial mess,' but, during the second term, on 14 February 1926, he wrote: 'the Sorbonne, as far as I am concerned, has been nothing but a disappointment.' Lack of system, the continual coming and going in classrooms during lectures, the inarticulateness of his professors, and the inefficiency of the libraries exasperated him to such a degree

that, when the year finished, he never again set foot in a place where, curiously, his most enjoyable attendance had been at a special performance of *Parsifal* given by candlelight in the Sorbonne church.

Academic disillusionments were more than made up for by the musical life of Paris. In this realm Douglas shortly became as infallible a pilot as the weekly *Guide du concert* which was his constant companion. He knew the acoustics of every recital hall, of the Opéra and the Opéra-comique, as well as those seats from which one could hear and see best at advantageous prices. Aware in advance of what was to be performed, he secured tickets well ahead of time, in combinations that permitted attending several concerts in a single afternoon or evening, at each of which he would remain just long enough to hear the part of the concert that interested him, before leaving for the next. On such occasions he usually invited one or more friends to go too, sometimes because they shared his enthusiasm or his curiosity, sometimes, mischievously, because they did not, but invariably because he eagerly anticipated talking over performers and performances in detail afterward. For Douglas, this was an essential part of the proceedings and to such discussion he contributed striking comparisons, his memory for interpretation being phenomenal. He had had some early musical training, and an accurate ear together with a gift for whistling with the clarity of a flute enabled him to illustrate certain points in a way both pleasant and conclusive. While his taste was eclectic, he showed marked interest in music of the nineteenth century, particularly that of Wagner and the impressionists; he now rapidly grew familiar with the works of Falla, Honnegger, Milhaud, Poulenc, Satie, Schoenberg, and Stravinsky, which were constantly being performed. A subscriber to the more classical Concerts Pasdeloup, Colonne, Lamoureux, and the Orchestre symphonique de Paris, he was also an assiduous auditor at recitals by such singers as Jane Bathori, Claire Croiza, and Charles Panzéra, the three leading interpreters of Debussy, Fauré, and Ravel.

Douglas was also devoted to opera. In the summer of 1926, he went to Munich for the Wagner Festival (then alternating between Munich and Bayreuth) at which time he heard *The Ring* and *Parsifal*. In Paris, he took in every presentation of *Tristan*, an opera which ranked high in his esteem, as did the operas of Richard Strauss, especially *Salomé*. But his predilection was for Debussy's *Pelléas et Mélisande*.

He became acquainted with this work in Paris, where it was intermittently revived on and after the occasion of the twenty-fifth anniversary of its first performance there, Mary Garden again singing the role of Mélisande which she created. From then on Douglas rarely missed a performance of Debussy's masterpiece. He was highly pleased when I obtained the score and never tired of hearing it played from, on the piano. It is no exaggeration to say that he knew and loved every note; each fresh recording of *Pelléas et Mélisande* was added to his collection and he was delighted when friends would join him, with or without the score, in comparing these various readings. At the same time, and with gusto, he aided and abetted me in composing a lyric parody, based on our personal experiences of French bureaucracy, which we adapted and sang to the music of the opera. producing an infinitely extensible melodrama to which we gave the title *Mélisande va à la Préfecture de Police pour avoir sa carte d'identité*.

Douglas' devotion to opera was paralleled by a similar devotion to ballet, which dated from his boyhood, when he was taken to see Pavlova. In Paris he attended the Diaghilev ballets, many of them new, most of them danced to music by contemporary composers. Long before coming to France he had acquired reproductions of stage-sets and costume designs by Roerich and Bakst; in Paris he saw and admired the work of these and other artists, such as Braque, Chirico, and Picasso, not only at the Diaghilev series but also at the Ballet suédois, the Théâtre Bériza, and the tiny theatre directed by Xavier de Courville, whom we occasionally came across in the act of transporting his own exquisitely conceived sets through the streets on a bicycle-trailer. Both Douglas and I rounded out our appreciation of ballet design by visits to the Bibliothèque de l'Opéra; I remember his excitement on discovering the calligraphy of choreographers' notebooks which are also preserved there. When later on he took up bookbinding, he would sometimes refer to the possibility of using such stenographic symbols as units in ornamental design.

The three dancers whose art most appealed to Douglas were highly contrasted. The first of these was Pavlova, the epitome of classic style, for whom Douglas' early enthusiasm never waned. The second was Ida Rubenstein, with her individual talent for exotic dance-mime, whom he saw create Ravel's *Boléro*, Honegger's *Amphion* and *l'Impératice aux Rochers*, and the *Orphée* of Roger-Ducasse. The third was Argentina, whose creation of Falla's l'*Amour sorcier* Douglas witnessed at the Théâtre Bériza. Her elegant and dynamic stylization of provincial and popular Spanish folk elements, an exact parallel to what Falla was doing in the realm of music, made irresistible appeal to Douglas' special feeling for a fusion of primitivism and refinement, a balance of violence and delicacy. He lost no opportunity of seeing any performance by Argentina, whom he eventually met and whose cordial friendship he enjoyed until her untimely death in 1936. His keen interest in choreographic art was maintained until his own death, as the National Ballet can testify.

Douglas' interest in recorded music, briefly referred to above, deserves further mention. In Toronto he had early developed a flair for recordings of out-of-the-way music, which were then just beginning to come into their own. He haunted the Gramophone Shop in New York whenever he was in that city, and during his last undergraduate years subscribed to the London Gramophone Society. These two centres, over a period of years, were the sole sources for records of bygone and contemporary works, until the opening in Paris of La Boîte à Musique, where Douglas quickly became a well-known figure. Various recordings of a single work he would assemble not only for the pleasure of hearing but also for that of cross-comparison. Some of those who shared such experiences for the first time were startled to find they were expected to listen closely. Douglas made no remarks while playing a record, though occasionally his long forefinger would point in the direction of the machine, to indicate the imminence of some feature referred to before the playing began and destined for comment when the record ended. He gave the same critical attention to both live and recorded music and to be with him at a session of either kind was, for his friends, not only stimulating but instructive, even influential. One of those who especially benefited by such associations was his sister, Frances Duncan Barwick, an accomplished musician, who, in large part because of her brother's interest and encouragement, studied in Paris and became Canada's first harpsichordist. It is worthy of note that although in later years Douglas gave up attending concerts, opera, and ballet altogether, he continued to collect and enjoy recorded music and to share his enjoyment of it with others until the end of his life.

Douglas' interest in the Paris theatre was at first mainly utilitarian. 'I really must go to plays, instead of some of the concerts' he wrote in December 1925, 'because it will be much needed practice in quick comprehension. I mean particularly at the standard theatres such as the Théâtre Français, the Odéon, the Vieux-Colombier, etc, where perfect elocution is a speciality.' Some two months later, 'beginning to feel confident about tackling anybody in French,' he expanded his theatre-going to include avant-garde plays at the cartel of little theatres that, under the direction of Dullin, Baty, Pitoëff, and Jouvet, were continuing, with extraordinary success, the renaissance of the French stage begun by Antoine Copeau. Douglas was enchanted by the diction of Ludmilla Pitoëff and, I believe, attended at least one performance of each of the many plays in which she appeared.

Among French moving-picture producers whose work he followed were Jean Renoir, Jean Cocteau, and, later, Jacques Tati. It was in Paris that he first saw Eisenstein's dramatic photography to which he often referred. Among films that he went to more than once were *L'Ange bleu*, *Mädchen in Uniform*, *Le Sang d'un Poète*, *Le Cabinet du docteur Caligari*, and *La Cucuracha* (the latter on account of Argentina who danced in it). He cared less about the content of a film than about its manner of presentation, less about a role than about the way it was performed. Himself a gifted photographer, who would go to great lengths in order to obtain a desired effect, he seemed to look out for and appreciate in films, skilful technique, effective structure, and whatever was distinctive in the miming or timing of a protagonist. Westerns, then as now the rage among a large body of the Paris intelligentsia, left him cold, whereas he kept an open eye and mind for experimental films, the scope of his taste in these being obvious.

Soon after coming to Paris, Douglas was welcomed into a Montparnasse circle that met regularly, in both the apartment and in the studio of two hospitable Canadian artists, the painter-etcher Cecelia MacKinnon and the bookbinder Agnes St John. In this cosmopolitan group, where new people were always turning up, Douglas became one of the constant visitors, among whom were, for example, the painter Helena Darmesteter, the violinist Jan Hambourg, the etcher Livia Kadar, the writer Dudley Poore, the critic Maximilien Gauthier, the pianist Mary Morley, and the Arthurian scholars Roger and

Laura Loomis. The most influential of these associations for Douglas was the friendship that sprang up between him and Agnes St John, whose bindings were, and are, prized in France, England, and the United States, though all but unknown in her own country. Each of the two new friends had a similar drily sparkling sense of humour and many interests in common, but Agnes St John was quick to perceive in Douglas the kind of taste, judgment, concern about properties of media, and meticulous care for detail that constitute the make-up of a master binder.

It was not long before she invited him to inspect her binding equipment at the studio, where she took pleasure in talking about the secrets of the métier to one who asked pertinent and sensitive questions that, as she said, were a joy to answer. To her delight, Douglas rapidly evinced a deep interest, not only in the mechanics of bookbinding but also in the history of its development, an interest which she did all in her power to further, by placing her library of books on the subject at his disposal, by visiting with him the bindings in the Cluny, the Arsenal, and the musée Condé at Chantilly, and by obtaining for him access to the less available Petit Palais, Versailles library, and de Broglie collections. I recall that Douglas was fascinated by the few extant examples of mediaeval binding, composed of carved ivory and cabochons, set in gold filigrane. It was on seeing these that he began making sketches, a practice he thenceforth maintained, of all details he found significant, in bindings, architectural ornamentation, or mediaeval metal motifs. I was present with him on several expeditions of the kind, both in and out of Paris, and especially remember one to Rouen where he confessed that the hours he spent drawing among the treasures of wrought-iron seemed more like minutes. Although ready to explain why he chose a certain pattern, he was not inclined to display his sketches and I for one came to think of them as just another secret of the métier, a secret that was to bear fruit, however, in the gilding tools he later ordered to be made from such designs, each *petit fer* bearing an initial, an heraldic or symbolic device, a stylized flower, animal, or other object, engraved in relief on metal, for heating to a precise degree in order that the motif or 'theme' be clearly stamped into the leather of a binding.

During the summer of 1926, although we retained a *pied-à-terre* at the same address in the rue Vaneau, Douglas and I separately made a number of journeys, Douglas visiting and revisiting various parts of France, going to England, Germany, Austria, and Switzerland, and incidentally taking in a considerable number of concerts, operas, and ballets along the way. On his return to Paris in the autumn, having now made up his mind to learn the art of bookbinding, he was introduced by Agnes St John to two internationally known and highly contrasted experts, the rather formal M. Noulhac and the completely charming M. Domont, under whose alternative able direction began work which he frequently described as taxing but rewarding and about which he wrote, on 9 November 1926, exactly a year from the day he first landed in France, 'The things to learn seem inexhaustible.'

Meanwhile, again thanks to Agnes St John, he found a more convenient place in which to combine living and binding, a furnished apartment on the first floor of 8 *bis* rue Campagne-première, the short street which Picasso and associates, after abandoning Montmartre, had made the nerve-centre of the new Montparnasse art quarter. It was a great change from the bourgeois greyness of the rue Vaneau. Next-door to 8 *bis* was the well-known art-supplies shop of the Guichardaz, a family whose red cheeks and

Binding by DMD, *autumn 1927*
actual size approximately 9¾″ by 9½″
17 different curves used;
2 dots / 1 straight line (short); 2 straight roulettes

blue smocks seemed fresh from their native Brittany; across the road, Chez Rosalie, a diminutive bistro, with walls hidden behind sketches and paintings by every modern artist known to fame, was presided over by a patronne renowned for having the most colourful tongue since Rabelais; at the corner, on the ground floor of a ramshackle building which had been condemned for more than a decade, was the original Jockey, a roistering *boîte*, which, to Douglas' distress, carried on seven nights a week below the sixty working-class families that had the misfortune to live above it. Rue Campagne-première was at that time still picturesque: white-robed members of the Raymond Duncan cult padded along in sandals and circlets; ballerinas from a neighbouring school hovered about, each balancing a tall vase, first on one shoulder, then on the other, to improve her carriage; monumental Gertrude Stein parked or unparked her model-T in the new little garage next door to Guichardaz. The Café du Dôme, frequented by artists and non-artists of every kind, was just a block away from the Jockey, down the boulevard du Montparnasse.

An ancient gateway marked 8 *bis* gave access to an ivy-walled, cobblestone alley, which passed below the windows of the MacKinnon-St John studio and led to a succession of courtyards and buildings beyond. Hither we conveyed the faithful gramophone, together with quantities of records and seemingly endless books, Douglas being a confirmed bibliophile. Not one myself, I am incompetent to speak intelligently of the finds I was made aware he made. New books were always appearing on his shelves, first editions and limited, autographed, or special editions, many of them published by the NRF and often purchased at Le Grand Meaulnes, a Montparnasse *librairie*, named after a book of which Douglas was very fond. Some of the volumes were intended for binding and now and again he would consult one or another of us as to the suitability of such and such a leather or motif. At these times Douglas made use of a mysterious vocabulary. I remember his amusement, on several occasions, over my repeated failure to understand his explicit clarifications of bookbinding terms. Finally, one day, when I reopened fire, he silently handed me a small parcel. It contained a book and a card. The book was *La Reliure, poème didactique en 6 chants*, by Lesné; the card read: 'I thought you would rather have it lisped in numbers.'

BINDING *by* DMD, *September 1926*
actual size approximately 4″ by 5⅜″

35   Robert Finch

La Reliure, charming in its tooled leather of the 1820s, still reminds me of the giver's appreciative acceptance of all types of binding. Douglas was both pleased and amused by the neo-gothic designs of the Romantic period, he could wax eloquent over triumphs of the modern style which had been launched by Pierre Legrain, but his greatest affection was for the geometrical, fanfare, and mosaic patterns of the French classical era, with their controlled exuberance, austere richness, or mathematical fantasy, combinations he was later to reproduce or modulate with consummate skill and elegance.

At the rue Vaneau, with few exceptions the only meal we had taken was a breakfast of rolls and coffee or chocolate. Otherwise we went to a restaurant called La Petite Casserole and continued to do so after Douglas moved to the rue Campagne-première and I went to the adjacent rue Notre-Dame-des-Champs. La Petite Casserole was an unpretentious but immaculate little establishment, near the Dôme, with paper napkins and glass-topped tables. It even had atmosphere: its co-proprietress was a *comtesse*; its best customer was a Matisse odalisque model, who from under a wide floppy hat looked out unseeingly with one blue and one amber eye; finally, its *plat de résistance* was a superlative porridge, about which Douglas wrote 'we and almost all their patrons have it, irrespective of the time of day.' While Douglas and I appreciated *la cuisine française* and occasionally treated ourselves, or were treated, to it, such a luxury was too expensive for students who preferred to invest their limited funds in other ways. I think, for instance, of a typically douglasian letter, which reads in part: 'There are so many wonderful things announced for May and June: concerts under Furtwaengler, Stravinsky, Koussevitsky; Pavlova, Argentina and her Spanish Ballet, the Diaghilev Ballets Russes; a cycle of the five Mozart operas, with selected international stars; ten days of the Vienna Opera, with Jeritza and Elizabeth Schumann; theatrical companies (I believe) from foreign capitals. In fact, Bayreuth, Munich and Salzburg are rather outdone by Paris this early summer.' I think also of Douglas' many pilgrimages in France; he had a passion for going to Chartres; in Normandy he several times visited the Mont-Saint-Michel, 'perhaps ten times' explored Rouen and its vicinity, especially the feudal fortress of the Château-Gaillard; he knew all the principal French romanesque churches, notably Vézelay, Moissac, and Souillac; with friends, he drove his little Renault ('Renny the Rattler') through the Massif Central and the Dordogne valley; these are only a few of the experiences he preferred to gastronomical ones, his sole indulgence in the latter kind, about which he good-naturedly allowed himself to be teased, being the absorption, at any time and anywhere, of his favourite *chocolat liégeois*, not one but several.

In 1927, sudden death deprived Douglas of the good friend whom he used to call his 'binding godmother.' In January 1928, he took a studio (also at 8 *bis* rue Campagne-première) and installed in it several important items acquired from Agnes St John's estate, including her big press. These he supplemented through the purchase of further equipment. He now obtained his endpapers not only in Paris but also from London, New York, and Berlin. Leather, about which he had become uncommonly well-informed, he usually bought in Paris, chez Jullien. Moreover, his first order of gilding tools was made and delivered to him at this time and from then on he began doing more at home than in the ateliers of MM. Noulhac and Domont, whom, however, he continued to see, especially during the summers of 1929 and 1930, when he learned edge-gilding and repairing. Meanwhile he also enjoyed the support and advice of Miss Lahey, of the Morgan Library, who worked always in the summers chez M. Domont. The association with MM. Noulhac and Domont was brought to an end by the death of both in 1931.

The preceding year, Douglas leased, for ten years, an unfurnished apartment, also at 8 *bis* rue Campagne-première but on the second floor, with a living-room which had an even better view than his former one of the same 'quite unsuspected big park of trees.' There were white walls and a fireplace of black marble with a gilt-framed mirror up to the ceiling. Here Douglas put two or three modern chairs, a small table, and, filling the wall opposite the window, a vast low flat divan which lit up the whole room with its magnificent coverlet of African material, woven in strips sewn together, each strip made up of an infinite number of small rectangles of clear reds, purples, and yellows. The only other colour was a full-size reproduction, on a wall to itself, of Van Gogh's portrait of Armand Roulin in yellow coat and blue hat. There were low bookshelves; the gramophone was conveniently near the vestibule where records stood in library order; there were also several heavy glass ashtrays of such distinction that newcomers hesitated to use them. This room, until 1939, was the scene of innumerable congenial gatherings and discussions that, for some of those who took part in them, remain unforgettable. With his accustomed thoughtful generosity, Douglas, when absent for short or long periods, invariably loaned or rented the apartment to friends, thus either giving them a holiday from narrow accommodation or providing them with the ideal solution of a housing problem.

Not long after settling here, Douglas placed in the living-room the sculpture of a young warrior, by Bourdelle. Until then he had always kept abreast of the many Paris art galleries; he had often expressed admiration for the productions of a variety of artists; to the best of my knowledge, the Bourdelle sculpture was his initial venture as a collector of original works of art, a role he was henceforth to play with remarkable discernment.

In the late summer of 1939, just prior to the outbreak of war, Douglas Duncan sailed for Canada. He never returned to France, but the wealth of experience brought back from his Paris years continues to enrich his country.

Barbara Moon

I researched and wrote this portrait of Douglas Duncan late in 1963, and it appeared in *Maclean's Magazine* in the issue of 4 January 1964. So far as I know, it was the only full-length profile of him in a general publication. When I began work on it I had met and interviewed Duncan on one earlier occasion, in connection with an article on David Milne. And of course I had some knowledge of Duncan's unique role in the art world, since it was this that had prompted the assignment in the first place. But I scarcely knew him in a personal way. In those days objectivity was considered a virtue in professional journalists and what I am trying to say is that I was as objective as I could be about him. And so, though there are references in it that are now sadly out-of-date, I have decided not to revise them or indeed, aside from some abridgement, to try to alter the record in any way. The truth is I grew to like him so much that I now wouldn't trust myself to.

Douglas Moerdyke Duncan, a sixty-one-year-old Toronto bachelor, is a very tall, narrow man with a shrewd, whimsical face and a swift, self-conscious walk that suggests someone practised in avoiding projections such as table corners and packing crates. He is the proprietor of the Picture Loan Society, which offers original art for rental by the month (at two per cent of the assigned value, minimum rental one dollar per month), and also sponsors about ten small one-man exhibitions and sales of paintings a year.

The enterprise is so modest as to be nearly clandestine. It is open only nine months of the year, and then only in the afternoons and one weekday evening. An exiguous weekly newspaper notice is its only public advertisement. Direct-mail notices also go to a constituency of about five hundred but Duncan wants to prune the list. 'It's too much nuisance and costs ten cents a notice just to pamper their egos by getting lots of mail,' he says tartly.

The actual premises seem almost deliberately concealed. They consist of the third storey of a dingy downtown building that also houses an accordion school and two studios of dance, and the street entrance, on a rundown side street, gives no floor directions and no hours of business. The stairwell gives no directions either.

The double flight of stairs that in fact leads to the Picture Loan rooms at the top is so steep that at least one collector, a downtown lawyer, sent word that, while interested in a specific purchase from a particular show, he couldn't face the climb. Duncan replied, in effect, that a *serious* collector could. On the other hand Duncan has been known, in a pang of realistic concern, to pack down a selection of pictures to street level to spare an ailing art critic the same climb.

For the faint-hearted the gallery itself is almost equally disconcerting. The display space – a narrow hallway and four rooms opening from it – is as formidably cluttered as a lumber room in a turn-of-the-century mansion, a jungle of paintings hung, unhung, stacked, piled-up, propped behind doors, and leaning against baseboards. It is marvellous for people who like treasure hunts; Duncan himself does not always seem to know exactly what is where.

The Picture Loan is never very busy, even at exhibition openings, when domestic rosé is *not* served. It is never very businesslike either. One young couple who hired a picture for the usually assumed period (five months) neglected to return it for so long that, like delinquent letter writers, they grew too ashamed. They have now had the picture five years and the only thing they can think of doing is to set up a secret rendezvous with Duncan's assistant, pay him what is rather more than the face value of the picture in rentals, hide the canvas in the general disorder, and flee. Duncan has never once dunned them for either picture or money, which is what makes it impossible to face him.

It goes without saying that the Picture Loan has never been a money-making operation since its founding in 1936.

In these days of the eight-million-dollar Canadian art boom, of carpeted galleries with glamour lighting and smart addresses and of much art-market talk by knowing people, Duncan might well seem an unworldly old party and his shop a quaint backwater. But to those in the know – to everybody who is *anybody* in Canadian art – Douglas Duncan is a Cultural Force, maybe even a Major Influence. For, like Sir Robert Watson-Watt in wartime Britain, Duncan is one of those eternally fascinating unofficial figures, a backroom boy. 'Duncan has been tremendously important,' says Charles Comfort, director of the National Gallery in Ottawa. 'Vital,' agrees Harold Town, one of Canada's top living artists. Johnny Wayne, of Wayne and Shuster, is even more sententious. 'When the definitive history of Canadian art is written,' Wayne said recently, 'Douglas Duncan will go down as one of the really great men in it.' Wayne was speaking not as a comic but as someone who wandered into the Picture Loan fifteen years ago and learned from Duncan that there were good Canadian artists who couldn't get a showing, couldn't get a sale, and sometimes didn't have the price of a meal. Wayne vowed on the spot that he'd hang nothing on his walls but Canadian art and has since built a very respectable collection, most of it bought through Duncan. And he has recently taken his first steps into more active patronage, having informally sponsored – and talked up a lot – a young comer named Richard Gorman. Thus, though he is not in Duncan's stable of artists, Gorman indirectly owes something to Duncan, which is one way a backroom boy exerts Cultural Force.

There are other ways. For example, the Picture Loan was started explicitly as a showcase for living Canadian artists and for almost twenty years was the only commercial gallery in Canada so to specialize.

'He, to me, is the *pioneer*,' says Dorothy Cameron. Miss Cameron has her own – chic, successful – contemporary gallery in Toronto and there are nearly two dozen more flourishing across the country. 'Without Douglas, none of us would *exist*,' says Miss Cameron.

Or take Harold Town, who is the top-priced abstract artist in Canada and has a growing international reputation. Town says, 'Any real interest in my work begins precisely with the moment I first met Douglas Duncan.' Town was a commercial artist nine years out of art college, had sold only three serious paintings, had never had a one-man show, and had never been given space in a commercial gallery when he bumped into Duncan in the doorway of a framing shop in 1953. Duncan looked at the print of a horse that Town was carrying and promptly arranged a Town exhibition at the Picture Loan two months thence.

In fact Duncan has launched so many now-well-known Canadian artists into the crucial Toronto art market that even a partial list sounds like wilful name-dropping. As well as Town it includes Carl Schaefer, Will Ogilvie, Lemoine Fitzgerald, Jack Nichols, André Bièler, Henri Masson, Kazuo Naka-mura, Robert Hedrick, and Paul-Émile Borduas. In addition he was in very early indeed with Emily Carr.

He is not just a good handicapper; he is very much an active bettor. And he unfailingly gives his help when it's going to count the most – usually at the discouraging outset of a career. For example, of the six prints sold from the first Town show, four were bought by Duncan for his personal collection.

Though Duncan's collection includes Emily Carrs bought for $75 and $175 that are now worth anything up to $5000, and a Borduas bought for $45 that would cost ten times as much today, his interest is not speculative or even status-slanted. Nor does he look on his purchases as philanthropy – 'I won't take a picture just to help out'; he says severely. But if an otherwise promising beginner has nothing Duncan wants to buy, he is apt to make what he calls 'financial arrangements.' This turns out to mean putting the artist on a sort of retainer under a range of tactful guises. Sometimes it's understood to be a mortgage on choice future output, sometimes an advance against possible sales and rentals, sometimes it's salary for acting as Duncan's assistant. Since Duncan is fiscally blithe to the point of scattiness, there are graduates of such arrangements who have

River in Europe
photograph by DMD

not learned to this day where they stand. 'I think I must still owe him money,' says Robert Hedrick doubtfully. Hedrick, who has moved to another dealer, is at a loss to balance possible sales and rentals on work still lodged at Picture Loan, plus unknown personal purchases by Duncan, against informal cash handouts over more than a year. He can't get Duncan around to drawing up a statement, either.

In much the same tactful way, Duncan also supports mature artists whom he considers neglected, under-appreciated, or financially ill-used. For example, he bought a great deal of work from Wyndham Lewis, the bitter and erratic British writer-painter, who was marooned in Toronto without funds during the second world war. (Lewis repaid him strangely in *Self-Condemned*, his scathing novel about his sojourn in the New World: the book was received in Toronto as a *roman à clef* and, though every major detail missed the mark, his savage and perverse account of the patronizing aesthete-benefactor was taken to be a caricature of Duncan.)

In fact, for an artist on whom he is sold, there is almost nothing Duncan won't do. The case in point is David Milne, the hermit-genius of Canadian art. 'Duncan would be important in Canadian art for the Milne thing alone,' says one knowledgeable observer. Duncan spotted Milne's work at a Toronto gallery in 1934, sought him out in the Muskoka wilderness in 1935, and in 1938 became his agent. For the next fifteen years he gave Milne an annual one-man show at the Picture Loan and for the last thirteen years of Milne's life guaranteed Milne's income by making purchases for his personal collection to augment regular sales. In addition he became so devout an evangelist for the artist that a volatile Slavic painter in the Picture Loan group, Paraskeva Clark, burst out discontentedly, 'Agh. Duncan. With heem it's all Meelne, Meelne, Meelne, Meelne, Meelne, Meelne!'

Duncan ran errands for Milne, brought comforts to his cabin in the bush, respected his fierce need for privacy by acting as a mail-drop, fronted for him in so intimate a matter as divorce and, astonishingly (perhaps because Milne was even more impatient of bookkeeping than he), performed as a canny business agent and an artistic auditor. As a result he has photographic records of every extant Milne he has seen, and intends to present this unique catalogue of artistic development to the National Gallery, along with his own hand-picked collection of 160 Milne drypoints. It will be a superb contribution to the

Canadian national treasure – and quite possibly the first real advertisement to the general public of Duncan's existence as a Major Influence.

After all, the measure of a backroom boy may be the power he has, but the distinguishing mark is that he wields it unofficially and unpublicly.

Thus it is impossible to demonstrate conclusively that, for example, Duncan has affected the composition of the National Gallery collection, or has nudged the Art Gallery of Ontario's purchasing committee into occasional shows of boldness, or even that David Milne wouldn't have been accepted as a genius without him. On the other hand, anyone who goes looking can trace so many links between Duncan and the operative figures and/or interesting developments on the Canadian art scene that his significance becomes undoubted.

For example, two phenomena commonly held to have paved the way for the art boom of the sixties were the start of annual art auctions by the women's committees of public galleries, and the spread of the picture-rental idea. Though it seems hard now to realize, twenty years ago most Canadians had never seen a painting for sale by a living Canadian professional, let alone thought of taking a look at the price tag: it was a kind of disbelief in the possibility of ownership that the low-priced sales and the idea of rentals overcame.

The picture-rental idea, of course, spread across Canada specifically from the Picture Loan Society, which was the first in the country by a decade. It seems pertinent to mention, though, that its earliest imitator – and still the liveliest of nearly a dozen across Canada – was suggested in Vancouver by the daughter of Duncan's old friend and customer, the late J.S. McLean of Canada Packers, whose well-publicized art collection was also, in a very real way, a public advertisement of Duncan's private influence.

As for the women's committee sales, they were first thought up, for the Art Gallery in 1947, by Mrs Walter Gordon. Mrs Gordon, who once sent an s o s to Duncan for two rented Milnes to brighten their temporary Ottawa flat, is another old friend and long-time customer.

Both cases illustrate Duncan's germinal influence on the artistic course of events; but it is also to be noted that both also contain suggestions of what many consider his most crucial form of influence: his creation or guidance of taste. 'He is unofficial advisor to *everybody*,' says Pearl McCarthy, dean of

Canadian art critics. The truth is that, when it comes to promising artists or the pick of a particular art show, an astonishing number of people take Duncan's aesthetic word. It is not only a matter of his good performance chart: there is just something authoritative about him.

In this connection, it is perhaps not unimportant that he is a rich man's son.

He is, in fact, the son – born in Kalamazoo, Michigan in 1902 – of the late president of Provincial Paper Limited. Duncan claims that until his father's death his own income never bettered fifty-five hundred dollars a year; still, as he puts it, 'I was certain to have a lot of money.' This circumstance offers a kind of reassurance to people that such a man won't make aesthetic concessions to commercialism. It also seems in part responsible for Duncan's antic record of statements unpresented, books unkept, cheques uncashed, and things generally left undone that ought to have been done. He has not yet got around to framing and sending out *any* of the drawings sold from a Jack Nichols exhibition of over a year ago. On the other hand he has not cashed any of the cheques for them either. The chances are that he will go on overlooking this formality even if he does get the drawings delivered. The chances also are that he has been sending money to Nichols, now in France, and that Nichols, having received no accounting of the show's proceeds, will have no clear idea if he is Duncan's debtor or creditor. Many people find this sort of thing maddening but a man who has always been rich may not understand this. What Duncan says, impatiently, is, 'For years I have had more to do than I could cope with.'

Since the activity is voluntary it might be considered a manifestation of *noblesse oblige*. Certainly even as a youth growing up in Toronto Duncan had a lively disinclination to milk his privileges. Upon graduation from a general arts course at the university Duncan took a job in his father's downtown office. He went to work by streetcar rather than ride with his father because his father always arrived fifteen minutes after the rest of the staff. In the same way, he never mentioned to his parents his burning desire to go to Paris. His mother, a perceptive woman, finally got one of his friends to confirm her suspicions.

He left for Paris in 1925, stayed till 1928, and kept on a flat as a headquarters for annual visits until the outbreak of the second world war. For part of the time his only sister, Frances, then a brilliant student of the harpsichord, was his companion. Paris seems to have been a central experience for Duncan, confirming in him both the strain of civilized romanticism and the strain of elegant irony that have marked his taste and his habits. It certainly confirmed in him a severe aesthetic – so severe, it is said, that he will not sell a Milne to someone he feels doesn't *deserve* a Milne; in fact he will not sell any picture to someone he doesn't like.

In Paris he apprenticed himself to, and in two years mastered, the fastidious and recherché art of custom bookbinding and when he returned to Toronto set himself up in business not far from the present site of the Picture Loan.

In 1936 Duncan heard that Carl Schaefer, a vehement Canadian landscape painter whom he knew, couldn't get his work exhibited. In fact scarcely any of the current painters could. Duncan and a group of his friends discussed the situation. One of them had heard of the English venture called Picture Hire Limited, and with only this name as a clue they ad libbed the Picture Loan Society. The cost of display space was to be met by annual dues paid by member artists and member art-lovers, and by modest gallery commissions on sales and rentals. There was one frill: regular one-man shows offered to the artist for about half the real cost, plus fifteen per cent commission. Carl Schaefer was given the first one-man show.

The Society lost two hundred and fifty dollars the the first year, which Duncan made up out of his own pocket. By and by he found himself running the whole enterprise by default and has done so ever since, to proportionately the same fiscal effect. He bound his last book in 1949 and since that time has been a full-time cultural backroom boy.

Like all proper backroom boys he is an enigma to the outsider and a character in his own right to those who know him. He has a characteristic and disconcerting habit of hunkering down suddenly in the midst of whatever conversation he is carrying on. He says he does it partly because, being six-foot-two, he gets tired of looking down at his vis-à-vis' head all the time, partly because it pulls his muscles pleasantly, and partly because it allows others to look past him to the picture on the wall. He wears his clothes till they are out-at-elbows and looks, according to one friend, 'as though he were dressed by the Neighborhood Workers.' Until very recently he drove a rusted old Buick convertible with the torn rear windscreen held together with diaper pins. Both at the Picture Loan and at home in the family mansion where, except for Paris, he has always lived, he has a tendency to put things down wherever he happens to be when he's holding them. His sister, Frances, once riffled through the top layer of detritus beside his armchair and found three letters to her from friends, re-addressed to her in Paris in Duncan's hand, but not mailed. They were nine years old. He has a passion for sweets – Laura Secords, fudge sundaes, milk shakes – and largely lives on them. On weekends he climbs into his convertible with two fruit baskets and a trowel and scouts the Ontario countryside for wildflowers; he is particularly keen on wild orchids and has identified thirteen varieties, none of them rare.

In the summer he heads north to the Muskoka Lake district to the cabin he built with his own hands; it is complete with pipes and plumbing fixtures but the pipes have never been connected. There he takes photographs, swims, basks in the sun, lays planks into a nearby swamp to go after Showy Orchis, and attacks the underbrush with secateurs. He once drove two hundred and thirty miles out of his way to show some friends a particular view, and has been known to make an extempore evening trip from Toronto to Lake Erie just to look at the effect of moonlight on the sand dunes.

Some of his friends are afraid that he may dwindle from backroom boy to back number, now that the art world has gathered its own organized commercial momentum. Certainly many of his artists leave, after a time, for one or other of the new commercial dealers with an exciting contemporary image and a streamlined accounting system. Certainly the hip new generation of collectors goes where the crowd goes, and can afford to buy pictures outright in any case.

But a genuine connoisseur with a business address will always have a place in the art world, it seems. Eight years ago an apple-cheeked boy from Larder Lake saw the weekend Picture Loan ad, wandered in with a portfolio of paintings and said his name was Cecil Troy. Duncan said the paintings were terrible, but told him to keep at it. Finally, a year ago. Duncan told Troy he was ready for a show and gave him one. Half the show sold the first day and three quarters was sold by the end of two weeks. Troy thinks this would come to about $1,350.

Duncan has actually given him $300, but has made Troy his latest assistant. Duncan may not be the easiest patron to have acquired; but for all the right, rigorous reasons he is just the ticket for, say, a budding artist from Larder Lake – or indeed for any amateur of excellence.

Looked at the other way around, though, Troy may be just the ticket for Duncan: he used to earn his living as a banker and, by his own account, has a very orderly mind.

As a start he's got a sign on the door and the hallway dusted.

Rik Kettle

Barbara Moon's story covers most of the background very well and is a good story. She refers to a discussion in 1936 about Carl Schaefer's inability to get exhibited as the starting point from which someone (presumably me) mentioned Picture Hire Limited in London, England. I do not recall the Carl Schaefer situation but it may well have been part of the story.

My own recollection is that I was in London during the summer of 1934. (I was teaching at Upper Canada College at the time and my wife and I spent every second long school holiday in England up to the war.) I came across Picture Hire Limited in Brook Street in London that summer, talked with them about it in 1934 and thought the rental idea an extraordinarily good one. I remember there were several Christopher Woods in the rental collection – the first I had ever seen – also some Duncan Grants, I believe.

Probably during 1935 I talked about the idea to a number of people, particularly with Norah MacCullough, and wrote an article for *Queen's Quarterly* about it. Norah was enthusiastic, and suggested we talk to Douglas Duncan, whom I had not previously met. This we did, but things took time to 'gel' with Douglas and it was probably not until mid-1936 that

Douglas agreed to become involved.

We ultimately persuaded Douglas to do something about it with the inducement that I would undertake some of the organizing and work involved! This resulted in my drafting the original Picture Loan Society pamphlet, the general statement of aims and objects and the rental terms; and getting together the organizing committee as listed. This pamphlet, incidentally, was run off in the Printing Shop of UCC.

As a matter of interest, some of us in the organizing committee (plus friends) did a fair amount of physical work in putting the PLS room and hall into shape. Quite a few nights we stripped the walls, painted them in light grey, painted chairs and tables, and put up those narrow iron strips which made the hanging and changing of pictures relatively simple.

During much of the first year or so of PLS several of us took turns being on duty on the evenings PLS was open.

Most of the committee were reasonably active in assisting Douglas up to the beginning of the war, and my own active involvement lasted until about 1944. I remember making special rental arrangements for groups of paintings, including groups changing every few months, to Ontario Ladies' College, Whitby, and Upper Canada College.

As an odd personal thing I remember that my elder daughter, on her first day in the Private Patients' Pavilion following her birth, was exposed to a very handsome Will Ogilvie on the wall, rented for the occasion from PLS. This became a conversation piece around the hospital for a week or so, and brought a few customers to Charles Street.

I am not sure when the twice-monthly one-man shows first began – I imagine just before the war. The first direct-mail notice I have was for Scottie Wilson who first showed at PLS in 1941; and there were shows prior to that. This was Douglas' own idea and was expanded when additional space subsequently became available. Many of the young artists who showed there were relatively unknown and the story of Douglas' interest and support, given in his own remarkable and unique fashion, has been well recorded. For PLS at Charles Street these shows eventually became the core around which the rental activity was built.

Scottie Wilson had at least two one-man shows at PLS probably beginning around 1945 – before he wandered off to London and became a 'star' for one

of the galleries there. You know the story. You may
not know that Scottie, somewhere about 1944
I think, arrived from Vancouver at my house in
Toronto about 9 P M one dark, wet, and stormy night
with a large bundle of some hundred or more drawings under his arm and said he had been given my
name by the B C Federation of Canadian Artists. (I
was then acting as national secretary of the Federation, with Lawren Harris as the president and guiding
force of this group.) We spent the rest of the night
on the floor wading through Scottie's drawings.

From an initial polite curiosity, by the early morning hours I began to persuade him to let me arrange
a meeting with Douglas Duncan. Scottie, however,
was only interested in getting his drawings shown
in some large ground-floor store window where he
could charge ten cents' admission (which he said he
had done in Vancouver), the idea of exhibiting a
drawing for sale was against all his instincts: sell
anything – never!

It took some days before I could even persuade
him to see Douglas, and a considerable time after
that before Douglas in his own gentle and patient
way persuaded Scottie to have a show at P L S.

One other incidental item. At Scottie Wilson's

THE PICTURE LOAN SOCIETY

3 Charles St. West, Toronto

———

Organising Committee:
Douglas Duncan, H. Garnard Kettle, Erma Lennox, Norah McCullough
Gordon MacNamara, Pegi Nicol, Gordon Webber

———

TO ARTISTS

You have in your studio a number of paintings which are a potential
source of income. Some of them are occasionally offered to the
public for sale either in group exhibitions or in one man shows. Why
not loan some of these paintings for hire through this Society? They
will be more frequently in the public eye with the consequent increased
possibility of a sale and they will while on loan provide a steady
return.

TO THE PUBLIC

You like pictures in your homes, frequently see pictures that you
want but cannot always buy them, or even if you are tempted to a
purchase you are not always certain that the picture will continue to
interest you over a period of months or years. There are times too
when a picture may seem to have lost the interest it once held for you
and you wish to change it. Why not have contemporary paintings in
your home and change them if and when you feel inclined by hiring
them through this Society?

*It is felt that the public would also welcome the opportunity of having
sculpture in their homes. The Society will be pleased to accept small
sculpture and throughout this pamphlet 'paintings' or 'pictures' should
be read as including sculpture.*

The Society believes, as the above remarks indicate, that a picture
lending scheme can be of service to both public and the artist. This
belief is based on the success that has attended similar schemes in
London, Eng., and in several cities in the U.S.A. The Society is not,
as a Society, concerned with 'groups' or with any particular manner
of painting, but is essentially catholic. The Society is non-profit making.

The headquarters of the Picture Loan Society will be located at
3 Charles St. W., and pictures for loan or sale will be exhibited
there from 2 p.m. to 5 p.m. daily.

The Society will hold its opening night on Saturday, Nov. 14th,
at 8 p.m. Pictures will be received from artist members on Saturday
Nov. 7th, 10 a.m. to 4 p.m.; Nov. 9th-11th, 7 p.m. to 9 p.m. and
on Thursday Nov. 12th, 10 a.m. to 9 p.m.

PUBLIC MEMBERSHIP AND CONDITIONS OF RENTAL

(1) The yearly subscription is $2.00.

(2) Pictures may be hired for any length of time at the rate of 2% per month of their value (minimum rental $1.00 per month).

(3) Pictures may be bought outright, or by instalments at the rate of 10% per month of their value. If the decision to buy is made within six months, the hire already paid will be deducted from the purchase price.

(4) All rentals are payable in advance.

(5) Pictures are loaned by the Society on the understanding that they will be taken directly to the borrower's home and remain there until returned to the Society.

(6) Pictures must be returned to the Society or renewed on or before the last day of each month. Pictures taken between the 2nd and 27th day (inclusive) of any month must be rented pro rata for the balance of that month *and* the following month. Pictures hired between the 28th day and the last day of the month will only be charged for the following month.

(7) Hirers will be required to collect pictures from the Society or to arrange for their transport.

(8) Hirers will be held responsible for any breakage of glass and for damage to pictures and frames while in their possession.

(9) Members must notify the Society of any change of address.

(10) The Society reserves the right to refuse to renew the rental of any particular picture.

(11) The Society reserves the right to cancel membership at any time and will in such an event refund the member's subscription pro rata.

MEMBERSHIP FOR ARTISTS

(1) The yearly subscription is $2.00. This subscription also entitles artist members to the privileges of public membership, i.e. of hiring pictures, etc.

(2) Not more than 5 pictures may be sent to the Society by any one artist. The Society will ask for more if there is a sufficient demand for pictures by particular artists. For practical reasons pictures should not be larger than approximately 30" x 40". Prints and drawings valued at less than $10.00 will not be accepted.

(3) All pictures must be framed.

(4) Pictures must be delivered to the Society and in the event of withdrawal of a picture the artist will also be responsible for its transport.

(5) All pictures must be for hire, sale outright and sale by instalments.

(6) All pictures must have their value and the artist's name clearly marked on the back. The Society will not bargain over prices with a possible purchaser. Artists are therefore requested to bear this in mind when stating the value of any picture; it should represent the lowest price the artist is prepared to accept.

(7) All paintings eventually sold, either outright, after a period of rental or by instalments will be subject to a 10% commission charge.

(8) Artists will receive their rental charges (see Public Membership No. 2) less 10%.

(9) The Society insures all pictures against damage, theft and fire both while in their possession and while on loan.

(10) Artists may only recall pictures from the Society if one month's notice is given.

(11) The Society reserves the right to cancel membership at any time and will in such an event refund the member's subscription pro rata.

Artists will appreciate the service offered by the Society. Artists have only to deliver their work to the Society or to remove it. The Society insures it, exhibits it, recalls it when necessary and collects rentals and purchase money.

If you wish to become either an artist-member or a public-member, please complete the form below.

- -

To The Secretary, Picture Loan Society,
    3 Charles St. W., Toronto.

                        {an Artist Member}
Please enrol me as {a Public Member} of Picture Loan Society.
I enclose my cheque for $2.00.

    Name. . . . .

    Address. . . . .

            . . . .

first showing at P L S, Erma Lennox (of the P L S Committee) and her husband Ingham Sutcliffe bought each other a drawing by Scottie for a wedding anniversary present. Douglas was delighted and offered to mat and frame them, which he completed after something like two years! Typical of Douglas, and typical of some of the things one remembers with affection about Douglas.

P L S, of course, after the first few years became entirely Douglas 'doing his own thing' and doing it for thirty years or so, long before 'doing one's own thing' was credited with any personal or public virtue.

My own interest right at the beginning, and I think this was shared by some of the others, was primarily in the picture-rental idea with increasingly substantial general public participation. Remember, at that time in the mid-thirties many of us were active and concerned with notions about the arts and the public. This concern led to the setting up of groups like the Federation of Canadian Artists (with Lawren Harris, André Bièler, and Fred Taylor as the prime movers); to the Allied Arts Council (Betty Hahn the driving force); to the growing interest in community centres; and to the Arts Council brief to the Turgeon Com-

mittee (Herman Voaden and John Coulter, very active in 1941). I could think of a host of other activities pointing in the general direction of artist-public involvement.

It was probably natural that I saw the picture-rental idea as something which could and should eventually develop on a larger scale with substantial public involvement. The obvious parallel was books and public libraries: there are hundreds of books one can and wants to read with pleasure and benefit; there probably are not an awful lot one can or wants to buy and own permanently. There are, likewise, not an awful lot of paintings one can or wants to buy, but quite a lot that have a useful, if relatively short existence. Why not something approaching the public-library idea?

In the early post-war years I occasionally regretted that Douglas did not really push the rental side very much and that the number of people who participated remained relatively small. On the other hand, it was quite evident, thereafter, that the total 'happening' that went on at 3 Charles Street West, which was really Douglas himself, was so good and right that it couldn't have been anything else.

It has always interested me that the picture-rental

activities that have subsequently developed here have not really had much effect on the general public. They perform effectively and usefully but have remained, as far as I know, fairly small, sophisticated, and institutionalized.

I suppose, though, that the whole situation is now totally different, because of public exposure to the arts through the massive visual communication opportunities, etc (for example, Kenneth Clark's superb television series).

Douglas took the picture-rental idea and built around it 'his own thing.' Today, in our frustrations over the increasing disorder, discomfort, and dissent in our affluent society, we talk about our concern for the quality of life! Douglas, sitting on the floor on his haunches and twitching his eyebrows, would probably have thought this pretentious: but he instinctively busied himself only in things where 'quality of life' was concerned, and would have found it impossible to have done anything else.

Will Ogilvie

No history concerned with the development of art in Canada, from the early thirties on, would be complete without referring to the important part played in this development by the Picture Loan Society and by Douglas Duncan.

Elsewhere in this book, tribute is paid to that band of pioneers and enthusiasts who conceived the original idea of the Society and put these aims and ideals into practical form. Douglas was one of this original group and eventually he carried on the work of the Picture Loan Society, virtually alone, except that, from time to time, he had the assistance of one of a number of young artists. These were sensitive and aware people and they helped to create that unique kind of ambience, which always surrounded the rambling rooms and corridors of the Picture Loan.

The sponsorship and encouragement extended by Douglas to more mature artists, is well known so that what follows is an attempt to indicate how important a contribution he made in his untiring efforts to seek out and encourage younger artists whose work he believed deserved support and recognition.

In the development of an artist, especially of the young artist, there comes a crucial stage which needs that kind of encouragement which ensures steady not sporadic growth, so that a proper maturing will result. If stimulus is provided at this stage, then creative courage follows, and both are necessary for the artist if he is to go forward on a path which often is a difficult one.

Douglas was aware of this and, in addition, he possessed a unique gift, a kind of 'inner eye' searching out those qualities he considered necessary in a work of art. This is a rare kind of perceptiveness and is particularly needed in the appraisal of immature works. If Duncan believed that a work of this nature contained within it the germ of art, he would encourage the young artist with as much enthusiasm as he did mature artists whose work he admired. In doing this he became a kind of mentor and the young artists showed him their work, secure in the belief that he would give them an honest opinion and good advice.

He understood and spoke a painter's language and they knew he was knowledgeable about art, both in the technical sense and in the aesthetic. In going to him, they brought with them their own gift, trust in his judgment. Time, of course, is the final arbiter, but I feel sure that the names of a goodly number of young artists Douglas Duncan encouraged will be found eventually, among those who have made a significant contribution to the art of Canada.

Douglas has been referred to on occasions as being a 'discoverer of artists,' a 'connoisseur,' and a 'collector.' I do not know whether he would have agreed with these descriptions of his very consistent efforts to bring about a greater recognition and appreciation of art in this country, for he laboured in many fields. It would be difficult indeed to describe, so briefly, a man who possessed his unusual talents and, with them, a pronounced and complex character which seemed, at times, idiosyncratic, at others, paradoxical.

That his work, carried forward over much of his adult life, has borne fruit, is evidenced in a number of areas. Paintings revealing a catholic taste have come from his own collection to enrich a number of galleries widely dispersed in Canada. Private collectors have benefited from his encouragement and advice and he frequently sat on juries of selection, so that his influence has been widespread.

I think it could be said of Douglas, that he knew art was to be found in many and varied forms if one had the eyes to see, but he distrusted labels and was too concerned with the inner truth existing in all works of art to be trapped by the fashionable or the meretricious. He had great respect for and a deep understanding of the nature of art and he sought it out diligently.

In concluding these observations, I find myself coming back to what perhaps was of principal concern to Douglas. I think this was a desire to share with others his love of art: to be moved by its excitement and mystery and to expand, as much as possible, the enjoyment and enrichment art gives to a way of life.

African Boatmen
WILL OGILVIE
oil on canvas
actual size $40\frac{1}{4}''$ by
$48''$
reproduced by
permission of the
National Gallery
of Canada

Paraskeva Clark

I came to Canada in 1931 and met Douglas in the first year or two of my being here. The French language was probably one of the main reasons of our meeting at first, but I do not recall at all how we met or who introduced us.

It seems in my Toronto life Douglas was always there with all our mutual interests, our love of painting.

In 1968, in mid-June, we had a large garden party and Douglas came. He looked well considering his frequent illnesses in the previous few years and he said to me, after an exchange of greetings, 'I am just putting a new frame on the first painting that I got from you.' It was my very first landscape painting done in Muskoka in the summer of 1931 or maybe 1932. Ten days later, at eight o'clock in the morning, the telephone rang and Andrew Bell told me that Douglas had died the night before. It seemed utterly incredible after so recent a meeting and not even knowing he was in the hospital. Many artists were orphaned!

In the thirties, when there was very little public interest in Canadian artists, when there were so few private art galleries, and when there were no funds for acquiring art work in the public galleries,

Wheatfield
PARASKEVA CLARK
oil on canvas, 1936
actual size $26\frac{3}{4}''$ by $30\frac{3}{8}''$
reproduced by permission
of the National Gallery
of Canada

Douglas Duncan was the centre of inspiration, encouragement, and spiritual and often financial help for artists, particularly the young ones. When, at the closing moments of the memorial ceremony for Douglas at Victoria College Norman Endicott asked me to say a few words, I said, to the dismay of some friends present, that we had just heard how many interests in life Douglas had, how he loved Proust, books, architecture, music, etc, but I don't think he loved women – and yet nobody did as much as Douglas in encouraging women artists.

In the book *Adventure in Art* by Lucy Wertheim, a gallery owner in London, England, there is a chapter entitled 'Nursery for Artists.' She writes, 'My gallery was often referred to as a nursery for artists; I certainly nursed a large number into recognition.' This quotation could describe Douglas' Picture Loan Society. That 'nursery' of his looked after so many artists, beginning with Milne, Jack Nichols, Emily Carr, Harold Town, Borduas, Carl Schaefer, Will Ogilvie, Henri Masson, Pegi Nicol, and many, many others from all over Canada.

In the war years Wyndham Lewis lived in Toronto with his wife. He was bitter, grumpy, and needing money. Douglas became for him the starting point of exhibiting, meeting artists, getting commissions and support. I remember we had a party for him and Wyndham Lewis was happy being the centre of attention and telling us about the life in London and particularly about Bloomsbury. In many ways I think Douglas created around him Toronto's 'Bloomsbury'.

How he worked in that 'nursery' of his! Packing, unpacking, photographing for the advertising of exhibitions and for invitations, framing paintings for out-of-town artists, hanging exhibitions, and being there with his constant cigarette and slow low-toned conversation.

In the last few years he became quite swamped at the Picture Loan. It was a jungle of packing cases, paintings, and prints, stacked on the floors against the walls so one could hardly move around. Poor Douglas – it didn't seem to bother him – he was not well. Far away seemed the days of our youth, his whistling 'Ia Coucouracha,' the gay parties we had.

A short time ago, I was talking with Morley Callaghan about this era and he said, 'You were lucky to come right at that time.' Yes, as for so many other painters, Douglas was my good fortune. He was the climate that was beneficial to my taking roots in Canadian soil.

Michael Hayden

Tonight I was playing a record for friends and I flashed on how Douglas would have enjoyed it.

I knew him when I was barely beginning to compose my own efforts (I was just prying myself away from art college), and he exposed me to literary and musical experiences that I would be hard to convince could have been obtainable anywhere else.

We seldom spoke of visual art. Hours would be spent listening to records I would have culled from his collection. We'd debate which store had the finest selection of records and which had the most informed staff. Often, as I was leaving Sam the Record Man's, I'd meet him coming out of A & A's. I remember being stunned by his having the original hand-written drafts for novels and poems by people like D.H. Lawrence. The feeling of reading the originals was not something one could experience in a school library.

The first time I encountered Douglas and every time to follow, at the Picture Loan, he was slung into a chair which appeared desperately close to collapse, one leg over the other, covered with ashes, and surrounded by butt-filled ashtrays. I believe he was training for the 'he who could smoke a cigarette the longest and not flick the ash' Olympic record.

The gallery was always too full of work that testified to Douglas' generosity and kindness, with the very odd piece of excellence stacked behind layers of mediocrity. Upon visiting his apartment, I found what happened to the finer work. He used one apartment solely to house his collection; he lived in another, also crammed with painting and sculpture.

I liked him. He was good to me.

He purchased works from me when others regarded my work as a novelty. He was attracted to my work as visual objects. I remember, when he purchased *Jazzman* from me in 1965, he told me he seldom, if ever, listened to the tape playback that was part of the piece. This purchase assisted considerably in financing my first one-man show at Gallery Moos. I'm sure he knew it would.

He attended every show of mine in Toronto, but always *after* the opening. He'd come to look at my work, not socialize. For this I was deeply grateful.

He seemed to find great pleasure in knowing creative people. I found great pleasure in knowing him.

Johnny Wayne

There is no doubt in my mind that Douglas would have snorted derisively at the idea of this volume. That sort of reaction would not only be typically Douglas, but typically Canadian.

As a nation we are anti-hero. Unlike our neighbours to the south, we are reluctant to indulge in posthumous sentimentality. We have studiously avoided the literary canonization of our great men. Rather, the opposite is true. Behind every prime minister stands not only a beaming mother but a Peter Newman ready to reveal him to posterity and the Book-of-the-Month Club as a maladroit dunderhead.

For this reason it is necessary, from time to time, to reassure ourselves that there have been a few great Canadians. Douglas Duncan was one.

Some day, when historians document that chapter in the chronicle of Canadian art that could be called 'The Battle for Recognition of Our Artists' or 'The Pre-Sotheby Period,' Douglas will emerge as a giant of his time.

He was, in an era of artistic self-doubt, a source of strength and inspiration, not only to the painters he encouraged but to the rest of us who sought out the pleasure of his company amid the glorious clutter he called the Picture Loan Society.

I can see him now, squatting elegantly on the floor, aborigine-style, in the famous Duncan crouch, studying a Milne water-colour or a Varley drawing and discussing its fine points.

For me, and my wife Bea, for whom he had a special affection, there were countless hours of laughter and conversation about pictures and the people who painted them.

Looking back now, I realize that besides having a hell of a good time then, I was going through what high-priced psychologists call a 'learning experience.' Douglas was not only a dear friend but a teacher, who in a subtle way taught me the art of enjoying art.

Every picture I look at glows with his memory.

THE

DOUGLAS M. DUNCAN

COLLECTION

Distribution of the Douglas M. Duncan Collection

WORKS OF ART

NEWFOUNDLAND
St John's   Memorial University

NOVA SCOTIA
Halifax   Dalhousie University

PRINCE EDWARD ISLAND
Charlottetown   Confederation Art Gallery and Museum

NEW BRUNSWICK
Fredericton   Beaverbrook Art Gallery
Sackville   Owens Art Gallery, Mount Allison University

QUEBEC
Québec   Musée du Québec
                                       Université Laval

Montréal   Museum of Fine Arts
                                       Musée d'art contemporain
                                       Sir George Williams University

ONTARIO

Brantford	The Art Gallery of Brantford
Cobourg	Cobourg Art Gallery
Guelph	University of Guelph
Hamilton	The Art Gallery of Hamilton
	McMaster University
Kingston	Agnes Etherington Art Centre, Queen's University
Kitchener	Kitchener-Waterloo Art Gallery
Kleinburg	The McMichael Conservation Collection of Art
London	London Public Library and Art Museum
	The University of Western Ontario
Oshawa	The Robert McLaughlin Gallery
Ottawa	The National Gallery of Canada
	Carleton University
Owen Sound	The Tom Thomson Memorial Gallery and Museum of Fine Art
St Catharines	St Catharines and District Arts Council
Sarnia	Sarnia Public Library and Art Gallery
Toronto	Art Gallery of Ontario
	Hart House, University of Toronto
	Victoria University
	Royal Ontario Museum, Canadiana Department
	Toronto Public Libraries, Central Library
Windsor	The Art Gallery of Windsor

MANITOBA

Winnipeg — The Winnipeg Art Gallery
The University of Manitoba

SASKATCHEWAN

Regina — The Norman Mackenzie Art Gallery, University of Saskatchewan
Saskatoon — The Saskatoon Gallery and Conservatory Corporation

ALBERTA

Edmonton — Edmonton Art Gallery
Calgary — Glenbow-Alberta Institute

BRITISH COLUMBIA

Vancouver — The Vancouver Art Gallery
The University of British Columbia
Victoria — The Art Gallery of Greater Victoria

FRANCE

Paris — Canadian Cultural Centre

BOOKS

TORONTO   University of Toronto Library
                                Toronto Public Libraries, Central Library
                                Art Gallery of Ontario

CAMBRIDGE   St John's College

BOOKBINDING EQUIPMENT

TORONTO   University of Toronto Press

Artists represented in the Collection

CANADIAN

Earla Alexander
Henry Almeida
Eric Aldwinckle
Ralph Allen
Robert Annand
Anonymous (c 1900)
Caven Atkins

Aba Bayefsky
Roloff Beny
André Bièler
David Blackwood
Bruno Bobak
Paul-Emile Borduas
Rowell Bowles
James Boyd
Alice Bradshaw
Fritz Brandtner
Victor Brickus
Bertram Brooker

Leonard Brooks
D.P. Brown
Janos Buda
Dennis Burton
Jack Bush

Emily Carr
Paraskeva Clark
Alan C. Collier
Elford Cox

Dainis *see* Miezajs
Russell Dawson
Adrian Dingle
Ann MacIntosh Duff

Nicholas Eekman

André Fauteux
Mary Filer

Robert Finch
L.L. FitzGerald
George Forgie
Michael Forster
Paul Fournier
Lilian Freiman

Gerald Gladstone
Charles Goldhamer
John Gould
Julius Griffith

Frederick Hagan

John A. Hall
Lawren Harris
L.P. Harris
John Hass
Michael Hayden
Robert Hedrick

Gertrude Hermes
Tom Hodgson
Mercedes Horne
Yvonne McKague Housser
Barbara Howard
Gerald Humen
Jack Humphrey
Lawrence Hyde

P.K. Irwin

A.Y. Jackson
Phyllis Janes
Alan Jarvis

Anne Kahane
Stanley Knapp
David Knox
Ted Kramolc
Cornelius Kreighoff

Richard Lacroix
Arthur Lismer
Don Jean Louis
Alexandra Luke

Thoreau MacDonald
Pegi Nicol MacLeod
Gordon MacNamara
Henri Masson
A.E. Mathews
Norman McLaren
Dainis Miezajs
David B. Milne
Betty Mochizuki
Charles Morrey
J.W. Morrice
Sylvia Morton
Louis Muhlstock
Cawthra Mulock

Kazuo Nakamura
Jack Nichols

Will Ogilvie
Oswetok

L.A.C. Panton
Robert Paterson
Joseph Plaskett

George Rackus
Charles Redfern
Dieter Rechenberg
Goodridge Roberts
Jurgen Rose
Robert Ross
Hanni Rothschild

Peter Sager
Carl Schaefer
J. Brodie Shearer
Clare Shoniker
Gary Slipper
Jori Smith
Philip Smith
Michael Snow
Ron Spickett
R.A. Stevens

Jocelyn Taylor
Tom Thomson
Gerts Tiltins

Oswald Timmas
Harold Town
Cecil Troy
Ruth Tulving
Stanley F. Turner

Tony Urquhart

Valentine *see* Waterreus
F.H. Varley

Shirley Wales
George Wallace
Valentine Waterreus
Gustav Weisman
Joyce Wieland
C. Winter
Elizabeth Wyn Wood

EUROPEAN AND
AMERICAN

Alastair
Emile Antoine Bourdelle
E. Gordon Craig
Stanley W. Hayter
William Arthur Heintzelman
Käthe Kollwitz
Wyndham Lewis
Mariette Lydis
John Martin
Zoran Music
Pablo Picasso
Sir William Rothenstein
Georges Rouault
Graham Sutherland
Scottie Wilson

This book

was designed by

ALLAN FLEMING

with the assistance of

ANTJE LINGNER

and was printed by

University of Toronto Press